A Guide to Pruning Mature Fruit Trees in Arid Regions

by

Orville Blaine Whipple

British Library Cataloguing-in-Publication Data
A catalogue record for this book is available from the
British Library

Fruit Growing

In botany, a fruit is a part of a flowering plant that derives from specific tissues of the flower, one or more ovaries, and in some cases accessory tissues. In common language use though, 'fruit' normally means the fleshy seed-associated structures of a plant that are sweet or sour, and edible in the raw state, such as apples, oranges, grapes, strawberries, bananas, and lemons. Many fruit bearing plants have grown alongside the movements of humans and animals in a symbiotic relationship, as a means for seed dispersal and nutrition respectively. In fact, humans and many animals have become dependent on fruits as a source of food. Fruits account for a substantial fraction of the world's agricultural output, and some (such as the apple and the pomegranate) have acquired extensive cultural and symbolic meanings. Today, most fruit is produced using traditional farming practices, in large orchards or plantations, utilising pesticides and often the employment of hundreds of workers. However, the yield of fruit from organic farming is growing – and, importantly, many individuals are starting to grow their own fruits and vegetables. This historic and incredibly important foodstuff is gradually making a come-back into the individual garden.

The scientific study and cultivation of fruits is called 'pomology', and this branch of methodology divides fruits into groups based on plant morphology and anatomy. Some of these useful subdivisions broadly incorporate 'Pome Fruits', including apples and pears, and 'Stone Fruits' so called because of their characteristic middle, including peaches, almonds, apricots, plums and cherries. Many hundreds of fruits, including fleshy fruits like apple, peach, pear, kiwifruit, watermelon and mango are commercially valuable as human food, eaten both fresh and as jams, marmalade and other preserves, as well as in other recipes. Because fruits have been such a major part of the human diet, different cultures have developed many varying uses for fruits, which often do not revolve around eating. Many dry fruits are used as decorations or in dried flower arrangements, such as lotus, wheat, annual honesty and milkweed, whilst ornamental trees and shrubs are often cultivated for their colourful fruits (including holly, pyracantha, viburnum, skimmia, beautyberry and cotoneaster).

These widespread uses, practical as well as edible, make fruits a perfect thing to grow at home; and dependent on location and climate – they can be very low-maintenance crops. One of the most common fruits found in the British countryside (and towns for that matter) is the blackberry bush, which thrives in most soils – apart from those which are poorly drained or mostly made of dry or sandy soil. Apple trees are, of course, are another classic and whilst they may take several years to grow into a well-established tree, they will grow nicely in most sunny and well composted areas. Growing one's own fresh, juicy tomatoes is one of the great pleasures of summer gardening, and even if the gardener doesn't have room for rows of plants, pots or hanging baskets are a fantastic solution. The types, methods and approaches to growing fruit are myriad, and far too numerous to be discussed in any detail here, but there are always easy ways to get started for the complete novice. We hope that the reader is inspired by this book on fruit and fruit growing – and is encouraged to start, or continue their own cultivations. Good Luck!

PRUNING MATURE TREES

MANY and varied are the excuses offered by the man who owns an unpruned orchard; he is ashamed of the neglected trees, and tries to justify himself by advancing what he considers, or more likely what he tries to persuade himself, is a good reason. One holds that pruning is little short of sacrilege, contrary to the laws of nature; another tells of h s fond recollections of childhood, and what excellent fruit he picked from the old apple tree, pruned alone by nature; another says it does not pay, and in his particular case it does not, for the chances are that the orchard is neglected otherwise. The only excuse that has any semblance of justification is that of ignorance, and that does not excuse the man who makes no attempt.

Nature's object is the production of seed, with provision for its distribution, and she is satisfied when a cherry is produced with enough flesh to attract some fruit-loving bird that may, perchance, drop the seed far from the parent tree. Man grows the fruit for its fleshy parts, and tries to improve these parts, as much by placing the plant in a more favorable environment as by plant-breeding and selection. The man who has the fond recollections of childhood would no doubt find them only childish fancies, as did the man who returned to his

1

childhood home to renew his boyhood coasting and found no place steep enough on which to slide. The man who cannot afford to prune cannot afford to grow fruit, and the man who does not know how to prune, must learn; the principles are not complicated.

Physiology of Pruning

To be an intelligent pruner one must know something of plant physiology. He should know the effects produced by pruning at different seasons of the year, how to make a cut that will heal most readily, and the influence of pruning on the fruit-bearing habit of the tree.

It may be said that in the inter-mountain states the fruit-grower prunes at his leisure, but luckily this conforms rather closely to the proper season, when looked at from a physiological point of view. It is generally conceded that pruning in the dormant season incites wood growth, while pruning in the growing season promotes fruitfulness; and, since our trees tend to overbear, it is logical for us to prune largely during the dormant season.

Although it is said that pruning in the summer season may encourage the formation of fruit-buds on tardily bearing varieties, it may have the opposite effect, unless performed at the proper time, and may cause late growth and unfruitfulness. To give the desired results, one must summer-prune shortly before the season of growth ends; earlier pruning starts new growth, while late pruning gives no results. The benefit derived from summer pruning seems to depend on the ability of the orchardman to prune at a time to bring about early maturity. In an irrigated section where soil conditions are easily controlled, the same end may be more easily attained, no doubt, by proper manipulation of the irrigation water.

Both the season at which the wound is made and the character of the cut has an influence on the healing process. The pruner should remember that all food material capable of healing a wound is taking a downward course through the inner bark, and that to heal well, a wound must be in position to intercept the downward flow of sap from the foliage. When a limb is to be removed entirely, the cut should be at the union with and parallel to the surface from which the limb arises. When limbs are to be headed-back, they should be cut to a side limb and not to a bare stub. Wounds naturally heal best when made at a season when growth is most active, but, with the possible exception of wounds made in early winter, and subjected to a long season of drying, the season at which the wound is made practically has no important bearing upon the healing process. The grower, who has a small orchard that will permit of such a practice, should delay the pruning until as near the opening of the growing season as possible.

The influence of pruning on the fruit-bearing habit of the tree has been briefly mentioned, but the following pages will show how a fruit-bearing habit may, to a certain extent, dictate a course in pruning. The fruits with which this discussion has to deal have two general types of fruit-bearing: from terminal fruit-buds and from axillary fruit-buds (Chapter VI). The first type of fruit-bud is well represented in the apple and pear and the latter in the stone-fruits. Trees that produce axillary fruit-buds are naturally more prolific and require severe

ɪ

pruning as a means of thinning the fruit. In fact, a system of pruning under which the tree with axillary fruit-buds would thrive would cause the apple tree to overgrow to such an extent that it would be rendered almost barren. The point may be more fully illustrated by comparing the peach and the cherry. Although both develop axillary fruit-buds, they differ in their fruiting habits; the fruit-buds of the cherry are seldom found on the stronger-growing new wood, and severe pruning, as practiced on the peach, would throw much of the strength of the tree into the production of strong new wood that would carry very few fruit-buds. We have said that in the apple the type of fruit-bearing is from terminal buds, yet many varieties develop axillary fruit-buds. Varieties that develop axillary fruit-buds and bear terminal fruit-buds on young spurs all tend to overbear, and require severe pruning. To a certain extent, therefore, one can decide for himself how much to prune by observing how the tree bears its fruit.

Treatment of Wounds

The argument advanced in favor of dressing wounds is that it prevents decay and checks evaporation, both of which might interfere with the healing process. While in our arid climate the first is hardly applicable, the second should probably be doubly important. Yet the matter of dressing wounds is not so important but that work improperly done is worse than no treatment. A good lead paint is one of the most satisfactory dressings yet found. Rather a thick paint should be used, and careless daubing of the surrounding bark should be avoided. Grafting-wax is a good dressing, but is rather expensive, and difficult to apply. Other materials have been used, some successfully and some disastrously, and the grower is to be cautioned about experimenting; better adhere to materials known to be safe and efficient. Growers often overdo the matter and waste time in treating small wounds. Surely a wound less than one and one-half inches in diameter is not worth bothering with, if the wound is properly made.

These suggestions apply to wounds made by the careless cultivator as well as those made by the pruner. Unsightly wounds and permanent injury may often be avoided by proper treatment of trunk wounds. When the body of the tree is injured, the ragged edges of the bark should be pared off to sound tissue and the whole injury covered with paint or grafting-wax. If promptly done, this prevents drying out of the tissues, and new bark will readily form, except on parts where the outer wood cells are actually destroyed, and in time this will grow over. Wrapping the part with cloth, or, if it is near the ground, mounding earth up over it, will often answer the same purpose.

· *Pruning Tools*

Every pruner shou d be furnished with good tools; they encourage him to do good work. This does not necessarily mean that he must have every tool on the market, for many of them are useless; it does mean, however, that the ax and a dull saw have no place in the catalogue of pruning tools. The pruner needs a good sharp saw, a good

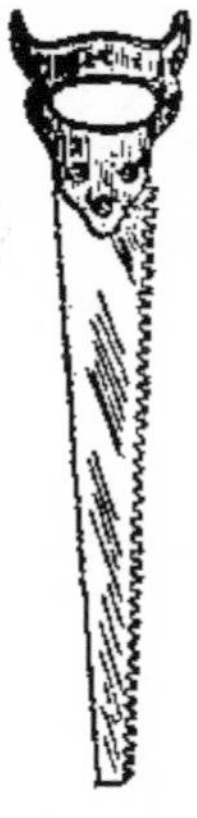

Fig. 32. — Pruning Saw.

pair of light shears, a pair of heavy shears, possibly a good heavy knife, and of course a good ladder.

The two common types of saws found on the market are those shown in Figures 32 and 33. That shown in Figure 32 is a good cheap saw, and will answer the purpose in many cases. A handier saw is shown in Figure 33. The blade is stretched between swivels and can be turned to any angle. It is well adapted to close work in the crotches of the tree. This type of saw, of various makes, can generally be bought for three dollars. The blades are not as frail as they look, and seldom break if properly handled; they can be replaced at a cost of fifty cents. It is really the best type of pruning saw, and should be used more generally.

FIG. 33. — Pruning Saw.

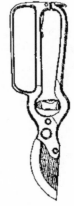

FIG. 34. — Pruning Shears.

A good type of hand shears is that shown in Figure 34. It is indispensable for light work. Various makes are on the market. Buy the one that appeals to you. A pair of heavy shears like those illustrated in Figure 35 is almost a necessity. They take the place of the saw in many cases, and will do the work in less time. They are used in heading-in limbs where the saw can hardly be used. The peach pruner finds good use for them. They work well on limbs up to one and one-half inches in diameter. The only objection the writers have to this tool is that the pruner sometimes gets careless and leaves stubs. There is a type of heavy shears on the market that has two cutting edges instead of one, but it seems to do no better work. The pruner finds very little use for a knife in pruning mature trees, and seldom carries a special pruning knife. Several types of the long-handled tree pruners are on the market, but they are of little value in the commercial orchard. The pruner should be close to his work, and with a good ladder and short-handled tools he will do better work.

Fig. 35. — Heavy Pruning Shears.

Pruning the Apple

With the young orchard well grown (see Chapter VII), the pruner has probably solved the most difficult problem in the pruning of the apple tree. The principles involved in the pruning of the old orchard are not complicated. Nearly all our standard commercial varieties of apple tend to overbear in the Far West, and one of the first objects of the pruner should be to overcome this tendency; the more prolific the variety, the heavier the pruning.

To be an intelligent pruner, one must also acquaint himself with the habits of growth of the different varieties as well as habits of fruit-bearing. Upright growers will require pruning to spread them, and straggling growers such heading-in as will make them grow more upright. The head should be kept reasonably open and well supplied with fruiting-wood throughout. The idea of the open head, however, can be overdone. (See Fig. 36.)

Limbs that interfere or are liable to form bad crotches should be removed and the main branches headed-in, as

Fig. 36. — Exaggerated Type of Open-centered Tree.

the tree indicates the need by overbearing or by weak growth. Moderate annual prunings are always to be preferred to heavy pruning at irregular intervals; these heavy prunings tend to upset a regular bearing habit, and may bring on an "off-year." However, if it should become necessary to employ drastic measures in pruning the neglected orchard, do not be afraid to use them, but do not make the mistake of selecting an "off-year" in which to do this heavy cutting.

Fig. 37. — Jonathan well Headed-in.

A discussion of the amount of pruning required by different varieties could almost as well be introduced here as that on the pruning of different kinds of fruit.

Yet the growth of the tree, and necessarily the pruning, depend much more on soil conditions; and while it might

FIG. 38. — Jonathan, growing Long, Weak Branches, due to Lack of proper Pruning.

be possible, it would hardly be safe to lay down definite rules for the pruning of any particular variety. Both the Winesap and Missouri (Pippin) may be classed as prolific varieties that require severe pruning. The Jona-

Fig. 39. — Ben Davis Fifteen Years Old and ruined. Such Loss may be avoided by proper Pruning.

than at the age of 11 or 12 years almost invariably begins to grow spindling in the top, and requires frequent cutting back to keep that tree in a thrifty condition. Figure 37 shows a Jonathan tree well headed-in, with stocky growth, while Figure 38 is of a neglected tree of the same variety and of the same age. These willowy limbs bear small

Fig. 40. — White Pearmain showing Type of Growth.

leaves and an abundance of apples that rarely come up to size, and the liability of such neglected trees breaking down under a load of fruit is well shown in Figure 39. Figure 37 shows how sprouts are largely avoided by cutting to side limbs. Varieties that bloom heavily but set very few fruits should be treated as varieties that overbear, and be pruned heavily during the dormant season. Varieties that refuse to develop fruit-buds should not be pruned excessively, at least not in the dormant season.

An idea of the difference in growth and fruiting-habit of two varieties may be had by comparing Figures 37 and 40, Jonathan and White Pearmain. The White Pearmain is rather a strong grower and a variety that does not bear heavily on young spurs. The fruiting-spurs are distributed along the larger limbs. Such a variety does not need a great deal of pruning.

Summer pruning is supposed to incite fruitfulness, but does not always give uniform and satisfactory results. Unfruitful varieties may be forced to bear fruit more easily by withholding water in late summer, or, better still, if the fault is known, plant them on a light soil; poor bearers are nearly always strong growers, and very often a shy bearer on heavy soils is prolific on a gravelly hillside. The Yellow Newtown is a striking example of a variety of this type. The growth and fruiting-habit of the tree determine largely what treatment it shall receive at the hand of the pruner. While pruning may not take the place of thinning entirely, it may be employed as a means of correcting the faults of alternate bearing and of overbearing.

Pruning the Apricot

In the general growth and fruiting-habit of the tree, the apricot occupies a position between the cherry and the peach. The fruit-buds are developed in the axils of leaves on both shortened, spur-like twigs and on the stronger-growing branches, both of the current season's growth. These fruiting-spurs of the apricot differ from those of the cherry in the fact that they develop no true terminal buds. The apparent terminal of the new growth is a lateral bud and may be either a fruit-bud or a branch-bud. It is generally a branch-bud, but it is not uncommon to find weak spurs bearing only fruit-buds, and such spurs, with no branch-buds to continue their growth, must perish at the close of the fruiting season.

The general plan of pruning the apricot resembles that followed in pruning the peach, although, as a rule, the cutting should be hardly as severe. The young tree is a strong grower, and must be put through about the same course of training as the young peach. This strengthens or stiffens the framework and develops a broad, low-headed tree. Normally the tree does not grow as much new wood as the peach, and it is often possible to do the greater part of the pruning by simply heading-in the strong growth. The pruning should be sufficient to keep the fruiting-wood growing thriftily and the tree well within bounds.

While to a certain extent pruning reduces the labor of hand thinning, it will not take its place entirely. If properly thinned, the apricot will stand much neglect as regards pruning, but proper pruning is a matter of economy. As the tree grows older it will need more severe pruning to force new fruiting-wood in the center. The absence of fruiting-wood in the center of the carelessly pruned apricot tree is even more pronounced than in the neglected peach tree. The top should be well spread and the fruiting area of the head maintained near the ground.

Pruning Mature Trees

While the season for pruning the apricot generally extends through February and March, summer pruning is rather extensively practiced on the Pacific coast, where the trees are headed-in as soon as the crop is harvested. This starts the smaller laterals into stronger growth, and they develop an abundance of fruit-buds. Limited observations of the same system employed in the inter-mountain climate suggest that it may not be without merit here. While this late growth is inclined to be immature and may suffer from severe winter freezing, it is more desirable from the standpoint of late blooming. Fruit-buds on this immature wood open four to five days later than those on mature wood. This may frequently be an advantage in localities where late spring frosts are not uncommon. The advisability of such a practice has not been fully demonstrated, and is given only as a suggestion.

Pruning the Cherry

The man who objects to pruning, vowing homage to nature, should grow cherries, for there is no fruit-tree of which it may be said that nature is a more efficient pruner. In fact, it is a common impression among fruit-growers that the mature cherry tree needs no pruning. This condition, however, is more largely due to indifference on the part of the markets than to an inability to secure results from pruning. When competition becomes more keen, fancy grades of cherries will gain in popularity and, as in the growing of other fancy fruits, pruning will be found to be expedient.

In the cherry the fruit is borne on one-year-old wood and mostly on short growths or spurs. An examination of the spurs will show that they differ from those of the apple in carrying both terminal and axillary buds, the terminal, with few exceptions, being a branch-bud, and those developed in the axils of the leaves mostly fruit-buds. Fruit-buds are also found as axillary buds near the base of the stronger-growing new wood. The cherry, then, has a fruiting-habit which would indicate that the tree will stand only moderate pruning. Trees overpruned produce an excess of strong new wood with few fruit-buds. In neglected trees the spurs become weak and spindling from constant bearing, the flowers are borne singly in the buds when they should be in pairs or triplets, and the tree produces a large number of medium-sized fruits.

The method of pruning will depend somewhat on the variety, but the general plan should be to keep the fruiting area of the tree as near the ground as possible; to shade the trunk to prevent sun-scald; and to encourage the growth of fruiting-wood throughout the entire top.

The sweet and semi-sweet varieties are upright growers, and will need some heading-in to keep them within bounds. The rapid growth forced by pruning must be checked by careful watering. Unless this precaution is heeded, immature growth will result, and young trees may be killed outright in severe winters. Like the Anjou pear, some of the cherries produce an excess of weak fruit-buds that fail to set fruit. When this is found to be the case, it is a good sign that the tree is not being pruned as severely as it should be. Heavy pruning in the dormant season will often correct this fault. On the contrary, lack of bloom is generally due to excessive pruning or overwatering. Occasionally we find a variety in which this fault is characteristic, but it may usually be overcome by proper handling.

Pruning the Peach

There is probably no fruit-tree that gives the careful, observing pruner as much pleasure in the pruning as does the peach. Results soon indicate whether the pruning is right or wrong, for no fruit-tree will suffer more from neglect, and none responds more promptly to careful treatment. This prompt response, so plainly indicated, lends not a little inspiration to the proper training and care of the peach orchard, and it is safe to say that, largely on this account, no fruit-tree is better pruned in our recognized peach sections. The practice is simple, and lack of courage is more often responsible for failure than complicated principles. As already mentioned, the peach develops its fruit-buds in the axils of the leaves, and the fruit is borne on one-year-old wood, being a system of fruit-bearing that makes severe pruning a prerequisite to successful peach-growing.

In pruning the peach, the object of the pruner should be to cut out enough wood to force good, strong new growth each year, to remove superfluous fruiting-wood, and to give the tree the desired shape. The mature peach tree should make an annual growth of at least 18 inches. With such new growth, much of the new wood will have to be removed entirely, while that remaining may be cut back to remove a part of the fruit-buds it carries. While some persons object to shortening-in the fruiting-wood, contending that it injures the fruit, the years of experience of our most careful growers recommend rather than condemn such a system of thinning. While it does not take the place of hand thinning entirely, it saves a great deal of tedious hand work.

It is hard to say just how much of the new wood is to be removed, or how much the remainder should be short-

Fig. 41. — Well-trained Peach Tree, Seven Years Old. Palisade, Colorado.

ened-in. Probably four-fifths is removed entirely, the amount removed from what remains depending more on the location of the fruit-buds. With the older tree it may be half or even more, while in the young tree it may be necessary to leave the laterals unpruned on account of the fruit-buds being nearer the tips.

It is a common practice to do the heavier pruning

early in the spring, leaving the clipping-back and thinning until later, some waiting until all danger of frost is past.

The pruner should constantly keep before him an ideal form for the peach tree; the well-grown young orchard at the mercy of a careless pruner may become ungainly and

Fig. 42.—Peach Tree, Nine Years Old, well Trained. Note how nearly it conforms to a Right Angle.

unproductive at the age of 10 years. Effort should be made to keep the fruit as near the ground as possible, as most of the fruit on a seven-year-old tree should be reached from the ground, and in no peach orchard should the picker need a ladder longer than six feet. (See Fig. 41.) The depth of the fruiting area of the peach tree

 K

will seldom exceed six or seven feet, and an attempt to increase this depth will only result in a smothering out of the wood below.

A better plan is to increase the productiveness of the tree by increasing its spread rather than its height. The ideal peach tree is one in which the top just comes within a right angle, or in other words, the spread should be almost double the height. Figure 42 illustrates the point very well. Notice how the head is well filled with fruiting-wood, and compare with Figure 43, a tree of the same age. With such a system of training, the first tree will be productive at the age of 15 years, while the latter, now 9 years old, must be rejuvenated by severe heading-in or be discarded as unprofitable.

There is no more frequent fault of the old peach tree than that of the absence of fruiting-wood in its lower parts. Such wood can be maintained below only by vigorous pruning in the top. The center should also be well filled with fruiting-wood, as space may be unnecessarily wasted by training the top too open; the open center is not a necessity in the arid sections, where sunshine is abundant. The fruiting-wood in the center of the tree will hardly appear as strong as that nearer the tips, but, nevertheless, some of our best fruit comes from short and apparently weak spurs along the larger limbs. Some have tried summer pruning (thinning out the new wood in the center of the tree), hoping to strengthen the remaining wood, but it has not given satisfactory results; too often it starts new growth that is immature and unfruitful.

It is seldom that we read a paper on the subject of pruning the peach orchard without finding some reference to the treatment of winter-injured trees. With the exception of young trees grown too late, or orchards in higher

Fig. 43.—Peach Tree of Same Age as Fig. 42. Note the Long Limbs with Fruiting-wood only in the Top.

altitudes or northern latitudes, such injury is not often experienced in the inter-mountain country. It is well for the grower to remember, however, that the winter-injured peach tree makes the best recovery when it has received a moderately severe pruning.

FIG. 44.—Peach Tree rejuvenated by Cutting-back or "Dehorning" the Large Limbs.

A subject more worthy of mention is that of the rejuvenation of the old peach orchard. The occasional loss of a peach crop by a late frost offers an excellent opportunity to grow a new top on the old peach tree. Figure 44 shows a peach tree 11 years old, two years after the grower had taken advantage of such an opportunity. The cutting-back should be performed as soon as possible after the loss of the crop can be ascertained. Severe pruning as late as the first of June forces rank new growth that develops very few fruit-buds. Rather large limbs may be cut if the bottom of the tree has some smaller growth, but cutting to bare stubs over two or three inches in diameter is hardly advisable.

Pruning the Pear

The mature pear tree does not require much pruning, nor does it allow lack of pruning to interfere seriously with its proper behavior so far as fruit-bearing is concerned. However, when the market demands that the fancy pear be from 2¼ to 3¼ inches in diameter, the owner of the old pear orchard is often reminded that the trees need pruning. In general, the manner of fruit-bearing of the pear is practically identical with that of the apple. The spurs are a little shorter and give the tree rather a more barren appearance, and, although some varieties develop axillary fruit-buds quite freely, the majority of the fruit-buds are terminal on these short spurs. The different varieties vary somewhat in their fruiting-habits, and a study of this character will indicate, to a certain extent, how much pruning each will require.

Apparently the grower accepts the upright-growing habit of the pear as inevitable, with hardly so much as an effort to train it otherwise. With proper training there is no reason why the pear tree may not be grown with a mod-

erately broad and low head.   Pears that grow in the tops
of high trees are too often scarred if not whipped off by wind

Fig. 45. — Improper Pruning of Neglected Pear Tree.

before they are mature, and, besides, it is too expensive to
pick them.   The shaping of the tree is determined mostly

by the treatment that the young tree receives; but a little judicious heading-in of the old tree, taking care to cut to outside buds or branches, will improve an undesirable form. Too often the tree is allowed to grow at will until it is out of reach, and then in a fit of desperation the grower resorts to such a system of heading-in as is shown in Figure 45. This system may be correct for the lawn hedge, but it is not well adapted to the pear, as is shown by Figure 46, the same tree one year later. By the time the pruner gets through with this tree he will have decided that it is poor policy to head-in pear trees. Had the pear tree been properly headed-in, the result would have been different. It is only reasonable to suppose that leaving stubs of large limbs which bear numerous fruit-spurs will result in rank new growth from these spurs, especially in an off-year, when the spurs carry a large proportion of branch-buds. When it becomes necessary to head in the large pear trees, always cut to side limbs, and do not make the mistake of choosing an off-year to do this severe pruning; a heavy crop tends to check rampant growth encouraged by vigorous pruning.

While some growers really believe that the pear tree will not stand pruning, we know of no variety to which moderate pruning is detrimental. On the other hand, there are varieties that require severe pruning. In spite of the fact that the Anjou pear is a favorite on the market, many a grower will not consider the planting of this variety. Yet a few of its more forbearing admirers have demonstrated that its one bad fault (tardy bearing) may be overcome by proper pruning. The young tree blooms freely and apparently sets very well, but before the fruits reach any size, the crop thins itself to almost nothing; even the old tree carries a very small proportion of its bloom to maturity. Heavy pruning in the dormant season will stop this

FIG. 46. — Same as Fig. 45 after One Season's Growth.

shedding and insure a good crop of fruit. The practice of the most successful growers is to cut the tree back each year and cut out some of the new wood that may have been forced by the last pruning. When once the tree begins to bear good crops, there is less trouble about its shedding.

Some other varieties are more tardy about blooming, and heavy pruning in the dormant season would only augment this objectionable character. Such varieties often respond to June pruning; and, if they do not, girdling in June will often prove beneficial. In girdling, a strip of bark one quarter of an inch in width and extending entirely around the trunk may be removed; but perhaps a safer plan is to remove vertical strips of bark one and one-half inches in width, leaving other strips of about the same width intact. If the wood is uninjured, these wounds soon heal and do not permanently injure the tree.

It is difficult to say just how much the pear should be pruned. The grower must decide for himself. The main object of pruning the mature tree should be to thin the fruit and thus improve the quality as well as to encourage more regular bearing. However, the grower must not feel that pruning will take the place of thinning entirely; to secure best results the two must go together.

The subject of pruning the pear could hardly be complete without some reference to the control of pear-blight. While it is true that when once the pear tree is inoculated with blight we must lay aside many of our ideas about pruning and cut to remove the affected parts, it is also true that, in a way, the tree may be trained to reduce to a minimum the loss from attacks of this disease. After the tree begins to bear, heavy pruning that may induce very heavy growth should be avoided if possible, as it is generally conceded that blight is more destructive to trees making rank growth. The majority of inoculations takes place through the blossoms, and one of the most serious types of injury is that occasioned by the entrance of blight into larger limbs through short spurs. Through these short spurs the germs gain entrance to the larger parts, and often girdle them before discoloration indicates their presence. It is the nature of the pear tree to develop these short spurs in abundance, and it will be necessary to remove them from the base of the larger limbs. Strong new wood may be allowed to take their places, and this may later be developed into fruiting-branches. Then, should blight enter these blossoms, they are far enough removed from the main limbs that the disease may be detected and intercepted before it reaches the most vital parts.

Pruning the Quince

While the importance of the quince industry in the West might not seem to warrant the insertion of this paragraph, the almost criminal neglect from which the quince tree suffers as regards pruning would move one to write a book. Among the fruit-trees herein considered, the quince has a fruit-bearing habit peculiar to itself. With the advance of spring the dormant buds on the one-year-old wood push out leafy shoots from three to four inches in length, and these are terminated by a single flower. While both axillary and terminal buds produce these flower-bearing shoots, the stronger flowers come from the axillary buds on the last half of the annual growth; terminal buds more frequently give rise to branches, or at most weak flower-bearing shoots. Considering its fruiting-habit, then, the quince should receive about the same pruning as the peach. While with some varieties the plant very readily assumes a tree form, others are, at their best, only a bush. A course of severe pruning for the young tree, however, will aid the grower in securing a desirably shaped tree.

When the tree has reached a bearing age, it should be pruned annually by thinning out the new wood and clipping-back that remaining to about two-thirds of its length. With proper pruning, the quince should produce annual growths from 12 to 24 inches in length. Too rank growth is not desirable on account of the stronger fruit-buds being nearer the tips, and in cutting-back such rank growth the pruning must not be too severe. The plant should be made to assume as near a tree form as possible, and then in addition it should be pruned with the idea of growing a goodly supply of new wood each season.

Pruning the Plum

Under this head is grouped a large number of species and varieties of fruit differing widely in their habits of growth and of fruit-bearing. Were it not for the fact that common practice seems to discourage the pruning of many varieties to any considerable extent, this would be a difficult subject to handle; no well-defined system of pruning would suit all. In their habits of fruit-bearing the majority of the plums resemble the apricot very much. Still, many of them, like the cherry, show more of an inclination to bear only branch-buds on the thriftier new wood. Like the apricot, the plums, with possibly a few exceptions, develop no true terminal buds. Except on weak spurs, the last axillary bud is generally a branch-bud that continues the growth of the branch or spur the following season. The fruit-buds are developed in the axils of the leaves on both spurs and on the ranker-growing new wood, the different varieties showing considerable variation in this respect.

The body of the plum tree is subject to injury from sunscald, and it goes without saying that the tree should be headed low. The young trees of most varieties will need cutting-back, and the tops thinned out, to develop them into desirably shaped trees. Some varieties will require pruning to spread them, and others, of a more straggling habit, will need cutting-back to inside buds or branches to make them grow more upright.

As mentioned before, the bearing plum tree, according to local custom, receives at most only moderate pruning. As a rule, the Domestica plums, locally represented by the various prunes, are pruned very little after they reach the bearing age. There are certain varieties that tend to overbear, however, and a certain amount of thinning-out of the fruiting-wood would greatly facilitate hand thinning, promote more regular bearing, and improve the quality of the fruit.

The pruning of the native plums is left largely to nature, although there is no reason why moderate pruning might not improve the quality of the fruit and lessen the difficulty of picking.

There is little doubt but that such varieties as the Burbank, Abundance, Satsuma, Red June, and others of the Japanese group, respond satisfactorily to rather severe pruning. In fact, they are more like the apricot in their fruiting-habit, and thrive under the same system of pruning. When neglected, they tend to overbear in alternate years. They should receive an annual heading-in and thinning-out to force strong new growth which makes very desirable fruiting-wood. While pruning as a means of thinning the fruit is not without merit in the case of the plums, it does not seem to give results comparable with those secured in the peach. The grower of fancy plums must supplement moderate pruning with hand-thinning.

Thinning the Fruit

In fancy-fruit growing, the necessity for thinning will become more apparent as competition becomes more keen. While the wisdom of thinning peaches is no longer doubted, growers are not so willing to take up systematic work in thinning apples and pears. But the time is coming when the fruit-grower will be forced to conclude that it no longer pays to grow poor fruit. Even now, the years that the grower makes a profit in shipping choice fruit are the exception rather than the rule. There are but few localities in which choice fruit cannot be grown, and wherever shipped, such fruit must generally compete with the home-grown product. On the other hand, localities in which strictly fancy fruit can be grown are limited, and competition in this class is more impartial. The competition is between localities which are probably equally distant from the market, and the one producing the best fruit is the successful competitor.

To a certain extent, pruning is a method of thinning, but it will not take the place of hand-thinning entirely. The production of a fancier grade of fruit is not the only benefit derived from thinning: it encourages more regular bearing; lessens the loss from the breaking of limbs; and gives the grower an opportunity to destroy insect-infested fruit, and thus check the spread of insects early in the season. The tree that has been properly thinned should produce a good crop of fruit buds each year, and if it has been both properly trained and thinned it will never need a prop.

While many persons have observed that apple and pear trees are inclined to bear alternate years, probably few understand the cause. Fruit-spurs with terminal fruit-buds, as those of apple and the pear, generally bear in alternate years only, and if the spurs are all full of fruit one year, the next must be an "off-year." Not only do the spurs fail to bear annually, but if the tree is overloaded, spurs that produce bloom, even though they fail to set fruit, may not be sufficiently nourished to produce fruit-buds for the following season. If the tree bears only a moderate crop of fruit, spurs that produce bloom but no fruit often develop fruit-buds the same season. If the tree is bearing a light load, spurs may mature fruit and develop fruit-buds the same season. Varieties differ, and while some are regular bearers under almost any treatment, others show a stubborn inclination to bear only alternate years. After the old tree has fallen into the habit of bearing alternate years, it is no doubt more difficult to get it back to a regular bearing habit. Off-years are not uncommon with some of the fruit trees bearing from axillary fruit-buds, but it is not so pronounced as with the apple and pear.

Thinning the Apple. — Fixed rules to be followed in thinning are hard to give. Much depends on the general thrift of the tree, and, as in pruning, the grower must learn much by experience. If we thin to encourage annual bearing, it will be seen that all the fruit must be removed from some of the spurs, and, at the same time, the number of fruits remaining must be reduced to such an extent that the tree is not overburdened. Some persons thin to leave the apples at given distances apart, but a rule fixing a certain space between the fruits will not hold good in all cases. If we were always sure the tree had been properly pruned, we might be able to give a satisfactory rule to be followed, leaving the fruits at so many inches apart.

A plan the writers have tried and found to be very satisfactory is so to thin as to leave a certain number of boxes of fruit on the tree. Suppose you decide that the tree should produce ten boxes of fancy fruit. A fairly uniform grade of apples ranging from $2\frac{1}{2}$ to 3 inches in diameter will pack about 150 to the box, and by thinning two or three trees and leaving the 1500 apples, actually counting them or estimating them as closely as possible, one learns what a tree properly thinned should look like. With these trees as a model, it is surprising how close one can come to leaving just the right number. We think it is possible, by careful work, to come within a box of the ideal. But knowing how much the tree should produce is where the experience counts.

Not many varieties of apple will require much thinning

before they are 10 years old, and at this age the average tree should produce about eight boxes of fancy fruit; some will produce more and some less. After the tenth year a gain of a box per year would be a conservative estimate. Of course the yield will vary under different conditions; and, while this is not a rule that may be implicitly followed, it is surely more accurate than thinning to a certain distance.

The thinner first removes defective or wormy specimens, and he should be supplied with a bag to carry the wormy fruits from the orchard to be destroyed; then those from the tips of the limbs may as well be removed, for they seldom make fancy fruit; and, if possible to do it and leave the required amount, thin to one fruit on the spur. June and early July is the proper season for thinning apples and pears.

Experiments have shown that it pays to thin apples. The fruit is improved in both size and color, the tree bears more regularly, and those that might break under heavy loads are saved. Some persons say it is expensive to thin; but, if one stops to calculate, he will find that it really costs no more to pick fruit in June than it does in October. A man can thin from ten to fifteen twelve-year-old trees per day, and the actual cost of thinning should not exceed two cents per box. It is true that the results the first season are often disappointing, for an unthinned tree may produce sixteen boxes of fruit that will grade 50 per cent fancy, while the thinned tree of the same age produces only ten boxes that will grade 95 per cent fancy. This hardly seems profitable; but the next year will tell, and it is safe to say that two years running the thinned tree will produce as much fancy fruit as the unthinned tree will produce of both fancy and choice.

Thinning Pears. — Methods of thinning pears differ little from those of thinning apples; the principles are the same. As a rule, the pear tree will produce about as many boxes of fruit as will the apple tree of the same age. The fruit is generally picked by installments, and it is possible to mature a large crop of fancy fruit; fruit that is small may be left until it reaches the desired size.

Pears running from 135 to 150 to the box are considered to be ideal size, and fruit for such a pack must measure from $2\frac{1}{4}$ to $2\frac{3}{4}$ inches in diameter. Pears larger than three inches are really not as desirable for the fancy fruit trade as those of smaller size. The fruit stands like a pear that can be sold two for five cents at a profit, and there is no profit to be made in selling the larger ones for that price, and they are not large enough to sell for five cents each.

Thinning Peaches. — In growing peaches, much of the thinning is done with the shears in the pruning season, but additional hand thinning is absolutely necessary. A good grade of peaches should run less than 90 to the box, and we may say it seldom pays to ship smaller fruit. A size that will pack less than 80 to the box is desirable. The young peach orchard that has been properly pruned will do well to average a box of fruit to the tree the fourth season in the orchard, and the yield should increase at the rate of about two boxes per tree per year. Unless the trees have been exceptionally well pruned and cared for, they will rarely more than hold their own after the eleventh or twelfth year.

The one object of thinning, as practiced with the stone-

L

fruits, is to produce better fruit. The thinning should be performed before the foliage gets too heavy and the pits begin to harden. By carefully thinning a few trees and estimating the number of fruits remaining, one can soon form an ideal to work by. The pruning shears may be used as a help in thinning, and such fruiting-wood as is not necessarily needed may be removed entirely.

Made in the USA
San Bernardino, CA
31 March 2019